ITSA MOUSE
AND THE CAKE HOUSE

Written by Toula Messer
Illustrations by Jimmy Messer

CONTENTS

ACKNOWLEDGEMENTS	5
INTRODUCTION	8
CHAPTER ONE	13
CHAPTER TWO	18
CHAPTER THREE	24
CHAPTER FOUR	29
CHAPTER FIVE	33
CHAPTER SIX	39
CHAPTER SEVEN	43
CHAPTER EIGHT	46
CHAPTER NINE	51
CHAPTER TEN	56
TOP SECRET	**70**
ACTIVITIES	78
SPECIAL MENTIONS	86
FREE GIFT	87

All rights reserved. No part of this publication may be reproduced, transmitted or broadcast in any form or by any means, electronic or mechanical, including photocopy, recording, or any information storage and retrieval system, without permission in writing from the publisher.

ISBN: 978-1-7399624-0-1

First printed 2021
Published by 100 Percent Publishing, London.

ACKNOWLEDGEMENTS

Enormous "thank yous" go to my lovely friends Heidi-Jane Hill, Diane Yorke and Sue Knight for the kind loan of your time and your eyes in giving my 'Itsa Mouse' story a good old read and letting me know your thoughts. Grateful thanks also go to Lisa Agasee and Marguerite Skinner for your generous support and kindness, as ever.

The most special mention and my sincerest gratitude goes to Tatyana Colombo for sharing the spark of an idea during much heartfelt laughter that eventually brought Itsa Mouse (née Liberace-Mouse) to life. You are an inspiration. Thank you so very, very much

To our oh so loveable Fairy God-Daughter and total ray of sunshine, Rebecca.

NOW LET'S MEET OUR MOST IMPORTANT MICE. DO NOT FEAR THEM, THEY'RE SO VERY NICE.

Itsa Mouse is the oldest and wisest, He's a bit bossy and always rightest!

Bigger Mouse is so named because he's tall, But it's mostly hat, if not all!

Fae Mouse is ever so gentle and full of fun, She's easy to spot by the giant button!

Hum Mouse is always chatting and singing, Dancing around clapping and grinning!

Our final mouse is sweet and bonny, She's the youngest of the gang and is named Nonny!

CHAPTER ONE

"This is NO way to live," cried Itsa Mouse.

"I just can't take it anymore!"

He was showing off in his white fur coat with the collar turned up, his wig skew-whiff, his sunglasses on and his sparkly paws in the air for effect.

Itsa Mouse was acting like a drama queen. It was a funny sight.

Itsa Mouse was looking for a new place to live. He and his merry band of now homeless mice had been kicked out of their last house.

The cold and damp December weather was too hard for them to be able to remain on London's streets any longer than they had to.

Itsa Mouse's gang of loyal friends had left all of their things behind them in a rush and squealed as soon as they had seen their human host coming at them with a giant-sized broom.

However, Itsa Mouse would never be seen dead without his wig, shades, fur coat and jewels.

So, he made a point of grabbing all of his things and happily marching past the human, who had been standing on a kitchen chair screaming at the top of her lungs.

Now, here they were camping out in a cardboard box at the back of Fortnum & Mason, a very posh store in the centre of London Town, above a warm air vent trying to work out their next steps.

CHAPTER TWO

"Look!" shouted Itsa Mouse to his gaggle of mice who were busily moaning about the sorry state of affairs they were now in.

"Take a look at her, why don't you?"

Itsa Mouse pointed ahead with his sky blue cane (his pride and joy – which was once a plastic cocktail stick he had found three houses ago), towards a young woman who was carefully getting down from her bike and locking it to a lamppost.

"Making another use of the cocktail stick, rather than it ending up in a river or the sea was the eco friendly thing to do," he thought.

The choir of chatty mice altogether quietened down and in total silence they turned as one, to see exactly what it was that their boss was pointing at and were none the wiser for it.

"Doh!" was the gang's only reaction sighed in a single note.

"She's got a basket on her bike! Hurry! Let's climb in and she can ride us all the way back to her warm house without us having to lift a whisker," said Itsa Mouse with glee.

For a moment his plan was greeted with total silence and then a babble of squeaks filled the air, as the little rascals caught up with Itsa Mouse's quick wit and fell in step (wiggling, it has to be said) behind their clever leader.

"Quick march!" said Itsa Mouse, not once looking behind him to check that he and his orders were being followed, as he stepped forward twirling his plastic cocktail stick like a baton.

He trusted that by now his mice would be in line behind him, knowing only too well that they couldn't stay on these mean streets without his help.

"Yes, Sir," said Hum Mouse, the happiest and cutest of the mice.

CHAPTER THREE

It took only moments for all five of them to reach shelter in the wicker basket, where the girl had luckily for them, left a half opened umbrella that they could sneak into and seek cover from the cold and the wet.

They had only just got comfy when the young woman came back.

She upset their joy by putting her shopping down right on top of them and unlocking the bike.

Mice are not often taken with the fear of small or dark spaces and right now they could not be, as the perfume coming from the box that was on top of them was far too tasty to ignore. It smelled just like Christmas!

During the ride back to the young woman's home, as the bike bumped along the road, Itsa Mouse and his mice became all silly with the strong scent of sugar, candied fruit and lemon zest wafting from the box.

"Mmm…heaven…" sighed Itsa Mouse.

"I'm in heaven…"

"Sigh, sigh, sigh, sigh, sigh…" sighed the rest of the gang, as they breathed in the sweet and spicy smell deep into their tiny empty bellies.

"Mmm...I want to live in that smell," said Fae Mouse in a squeaky voice.

"Think what it would be like to wake up to that every day!" said Bigger Mouse.

CHAPTER FOUR

Their sweet-smelling ride came to an end just as the mice were all falling asleep and into dreams of living in a Christmas smelling Wonderland.

The young lady hopped off her bike and leaned it carefully against a damp wall.

Itsa Mouse felt himself slide backwards under the magic box, making a 'shirrrr' sound against the inside of the brolly that he and his merry band of mice were trapped in.

"Wheeeeee!"

Itsa Mouse's chums were having a grand old time slipping and sliding with each other but this was no time to be playing around.

Their lives rested on what they did next. Or rather, what their master Itsa Mouse said they should do next.

"Quick smart gang – we have to get inside that box or we'll be left outside here, in the freezing cold!"

The mice didn't need to be told twice.

It wasn't every day that you were told by your leader to make your dreams come true.

Each tiny mouse, eager to find a way into this dream filled box, started wildly looking for a way in.

CHAPTER FIVE

It seemed that the 'smell' was coming from a plastic-covered lump that at such short notice was very hard to break into, but the outer wrapper was far easier to gain access to.

Nonny, the smallest mouse made herself as flat as she could and squeezed in through a gap in the cardboard.

Then, by using all of her mousely might, she started to pull her next smallest buddy in through the gap beside her.

Within seconds, all of these hungry mice had squeezed themselves into the box that the young woman then reached out for.

Even Itsa Mouse made it into the box just in time, but alas

his teeny tiny sunglasses were knocked off his pink pointy nose in the process.

"Help me! Help me!

I can't see," cried Itsa Mouse all upset. His sunglasses weren't

just for show by the way; Itsa Mouse is a very special kind of mouse.

He is albino – meaning that he is very special because he was born with pink skin, pure white fur and pink eyes that sadly don't see too well, especially in bright light.

Having no colour in his fur and skin also means that he has to keep out of the sun in case he burns, which is why he wears a fur coat to keep him safe; it is his pride and joy.

Without missing a beat, Itsa Mouse's band of gay and loyal mice were on the case of the missing shades and set about picking them up from where they had fallen.

In no time at all, due to the finding skills and love of his friends, Itsa Mouse's sunglasses were back upon his pointy pink nose and the world around him was all rosy once again.

Trapped together inside the Christmas smelling package, the mice were becoming as nutty as a fruit cake, from being so close to their wildest dream: dessert, with Itsa Mouse showing the fruitiest behaviour.

He was happily hugging all of his friends; it felt as though they were suddenly living in a candy cloud.

Just being out of the damp and frozen rain that they had become used to recently was a dream come true to them.

CHAPTER SIX

Inside the house, as the young woman placed the box down, Itsa Mouse put his tiny paw to his lips and told his gang to "shhh!"

He then put on his listening ears and waited until he could hear her footsteps walking away.

Soon there was complete and gentle silence. Not even a peep from a mouse could be heard.

Feeling safe, Itsa Mouse asked his team to quietly follow him as he made his way sneakily out of the box and onto a wooden table.

Itsa Mouse had learned when living in many of his earlier

homes, that this was the room people called the kitchen.

He had heard it said that it was the heart of the home, and Itsa Mouse could not agree more.

He knew it was where they kept all of their food, which made his heart full of joy.

"Oh, happy days!" sang Itsa Mouse to himself.

All of a sudden Itsa Mouse heard footsteps coming back towards the kitchen, so the mice made a mad dash to the box and snuck into it without a second to spare.

"Hmm. I thought I saw something," they heard the young woman say.

CHAPTER SEVEN

The mice all held their breath and each other, scared that they had been seen and that the game was up.

The next five seconds were the longest they had ever known.

Five. Four. Three. Two. One.

Lift-off! The box they were all hiding in was taken off of the table. As they were carried around, it felt like they were being shaken from their boots.

In fact, the lady had put the box under her arm to keep it safe, whilst she opened a small set of steps and climbed up them.

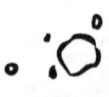

The mice heard the squeak of a hinge that needed a dab of oil and then felt their new home be placed gently down.

The squeak upset their tiny ears for a second time as the girl closed the cupboard door and then all was quiet on the dresser front.

CHAPTER EIGHT

A week and a half went by without any extra drama, as the mice got used to their new home and the comings and goings of their landlady.

Itsa Mouse and his furry bunch made merry after dark in this new house and ran around all over the place, doing their best to leave things as they found them.

In the living room, they found a rather large tree.

It smelled very strongly of pine and had loads of branches for them to climb and jump around on.

It was like a fun-park and many hours were spent racing each other to the top

and partying around as lights flashed on and off in so many bright colours. It was such a treat. They had never before had such fun.

The young woman, even though she was one of their tidiest ever landladies, clearing up and washing up after every meal, did every now and then leave behind a crumb of the tastiest foods for them to find, which sent them into a state of bliss.

They found crumbs of walnuts, most likely from the bowl of nuts sitting in their shiny shells, on the coffee table.

One day they even found a whole square of chocolate covered mint that had been left inside a small black paper wrapper, one of many it seemed, inside a long green box.

For the first time ever, they were not too worried about having to search for food.

Their little Christmas smelling nest had been giving them all enough eats to fill them up, as they nibbled away a little bit more each day.

As we know, all good things must come to an end. And so it was.

CHAPTER NINE

The day started just like any other. The mice were woken up by the ticking of the heaters growing as they got hotter and hotter in the early hours of the morning.

Coming from the houses next door they could hear shrieks of delight and the hurried footsteps of children.

Outside though, it was quiet. So very quiet, as all sounds were dulled by a thick frozen carpet of snow and flakes falling fast all around.

It was such a pretty sight to see, but alas, the mice had to be quick-smart as the landlady-girl was already coming down the stairs and heading for the kitchen.

Itsa Mouse had a bad feeling

about today. Something was in the air.

"Tick tock, team!!

We have a doodle-bug in our midst! Time to get back to the bunker before we have a shaky do!"

As usual, the little army didn't need warning twice, and marched in time back to safety, in their box in the cupboard at the top of the dresser.

For some reason this morning, there was a great deal more noise to be heard from their hiding place going on in the kitchen.

Pans were being banged, taps were running, things were being chopped up.

It was cooking music, and even though they had to stay

put in their hiding place, the mice became rather excited the more that they sniffed all the amazing food smells that were being made.

  Hours went by, during which the little critters ate and slept, ate and slept and then…all of a sudden they sat up wide awake at the same time.

  "Whaaaaat?!"

CHAPTER TEN

"Eek!"

The now chubby rodents squealed loudly all at once in shock. They had eaten every last crumb of their Christmas smelling home.

They were sitting in the middle of a very creased plastic empty wrapper inside a cardboard box… and you know how hungry mice can get. Very.

It was clear that there were some tasty treats being made out there in the kitchen but how would they ever get to them whilst 'madam' was so close by?

"Ding Dong! Ding Dong!"

Saved by the bell? Perhaps. The young lady shouted

loudly, "It's okay Mum, the door is open, you can just push it!"

"I'm in the kitchen! Great timing! Everything is in the oven and will be ready in just over an hour."

Oh no.

The mice would have to stay put for now.

"Hi Mum! Hi Dad! It's so lovely to see you."

"Do sit down. Can I pour you a little glass of bubbles, or would you prefer a cuppa to warm you up?"

"Ooh, a cuppa would be perfect, darling! We haven't had any breakfast yet."

"We wanted to get here as quickly as we could and help

you but it looks like you have it all under control."

"I don't suppose you have any of that wonderful cake that we so loved last year?!"

"A toasted slice of that with butter and a cuppa would be just the ticket!"

"Oh, the Panettone! Yes, I bought one just for you," said the girl, happy with her forward thinking.

With that, she got the set of steps from the cupboard under the stairs, placed them against the dresser and reached up into the cupboard at the very top.

The mice, all frozen with fear, could do nothing at all, as they felt her pick up the now empty box that they were sitting in and then place it on the table.

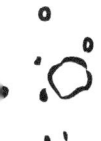

Silence.

More silence.

Even more silence.

"Hmm."

"That doesn't look right, does it love?" said Dad.

Itsa Mouse and the rest of his hairy friends knew what was coming next.

"Stand back whilst I open it," said Dad.

"Perhaps you should take it outside first?" said Mum, being smart.

"Okay, love," said Dad as he slowly picked up the box with the very tips of his fingers, as if it was a bomb that could go 'Bang!' at any moment.

The young woman fumbled with the key to the back door and then it was open.

A whoosh of freezing cold air filled the kitchen and it got even more icy as Dad stepped outside with the box.

No longer was the box Christmas smelling, or filled with tasty Panettone.

It was filled with five very plump and now heavy mice.

"Oh, you've got to come and see this," chuckled Dad as he looked at the round-bellied mice.

"Get that thing away from me!" squealed Mum as she looked at the chubby mice.

"Ewwwww!" spat out the girl as she looked at the tubby mice.

Without any warning at all, the girl squeamishly picked up the cake-less box by one of its corners, holding it as far away from herself as possible.

She then lifted the lid of her composting bin and threw the box inside, loudly clanging the metal lid down with a big gong sound.

"Oooooooh!" said Itsa mouse, as his eyes quickly adjusted to the darkness!

"What a wonderful gift! This new place is just perfect. It's so warm and dry and...look!" he said, as he turned all around, his tiny nose twitching as he sniffed the air.

"Our new home is filled to the brim with yummy foodstuffs!"

The high-pitched "squees" of very excited mice now filled the garden.

"Merry Christmas, love!" said Dad, sitting himself back down at the kitchen table.

"Perhaps we can have a couple of boiled eggs and soldiers instead?"

The End...or is it?

TOP SECRET!
SNEAK PEEK OF BOOK TWO

ITSA MOUSE BIN AND GONE

CHAPTER ONE

"Phew! That was a close call!" said Itsa Mouse, as he snuggled deeper into the pile of peelings. He was so happy.

"Just imagine that! One minute we were in an empty cake box with no crumbs left and the next we were dropped into this world of delights!"

The other mice, too busy munching on leftovers, replied with squeaky "oohs!" and "aahs!"

"What a Christmas this has turned out to be!" said Itsa Mouse, full of joy.

Itsa Mouse and his mouse friends: Nonny Mouse, Fae Mouse, Bigger Mouse and Hum Mouse were often homeless. They were soon found in every home that they moved into, so had to leave. Or were forced to leave.

The people in those homes were not at all happy to see the mice and quickly sent them packing. Sometimes they were swept out with a big, scratchy broom and at other times, like the most recent time, they were dropped or pushed from a great height.

However, this time they had been dropped from a great height into an almost full compost bin that was warm, smelly and full of tasty things to eat. It was wonderful!

Very soon all of the mice were fast asleep in their new home, warm under blankets made of cabbage leaves, dreaming of eating yummy carrot tops and Brussell sprouts. Not only were they now filled with food, but they were also filled with a feeling called gratitude. Gratitude is when you are so thankful for all of the good things that you have in your life, that even when the rest of your life is not perfect you still feel glad.

Outside of their new compost-bin-home, the world

was so quiet. Loads of snow had fallen from the white sky onto the ground to create a thick frozen carpet that ate up all of the noise. There was so much snow that all of the local children could build snowmen in their gardens and in the local parks if they wanted to. It had turned out to be the most perfect Christmas Day for these merry mice!

Itsa Mouse and his friends were so joyful in the garden bin that they soon forgot how difficult life had been for them when they were homeless

some weeks ago now.

Every day the girl whose house they had been living in before being dropped into the bin, now dropped fresh food and treats into their new bin-home, which they gobbled down greedily. Except for the onions. Onions did not make them happy at all.

They were all so contented. Hum Mouse would hum tunes all day long. Nonny Mouse and Fae Mouse would dance and twirl. Bigger Mouse would sit back with his paws behind his head, tipping his top hat to one side, and his little legs crossed as he thought about how great life was. Itsa Mouse also joined in with the humming, the dancing, twirling and the relaxing but when all of the others had all gone to sleep, he worried.

The bin-house that they had been living in for the past few weeks was now getting so full that their little pink pointy noses were squashed right up against the inside of the cold, metal lid when it was shut. The mice ate so much of the food that was being poured into

the bin but try as they might, they could not keep up. Nor could they keep the level of the rubbish down so that they had any room to move around.

Itsa Mouse knew something big was about to happen but didn't know what and didn't know when. He didn't want his little furry friends to also be worried, so he kept his worries to himself.

TO BE CONTINUED...

HOW TO DRAW ITSA MOUSE!

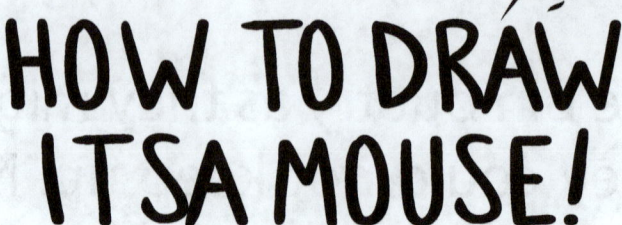

START BY GRABBING YOUR PENCIL & PAPER!

STEP 1.

DRAW A LINE. THEN DRAW A CIRCLE AT THE TOP OF IT.

SPLIT THAT CIRLE INTO THREE AND YOU SHOULD END UP WITH A LOLLYPOP SHAPE!

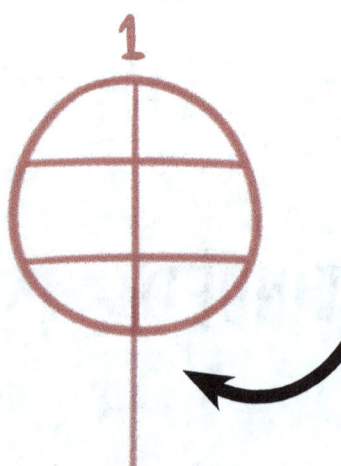

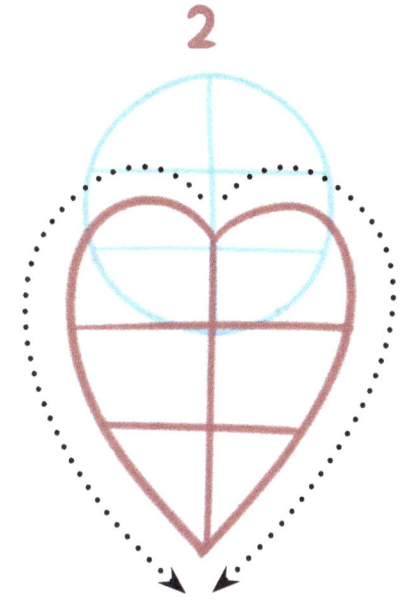

STEP 2.

NOW DRAW A HEART SHAPE, USING THE CENTRE AND SECOND LINES OF THE CIRCLE. DRAW ONE SIDE AT A TIME. NOW SPLIT THE HEART INTO THIRDS.

STEP 3.

NOW ADD THE EYEBROWS, THE MOUTH AND TEETH.

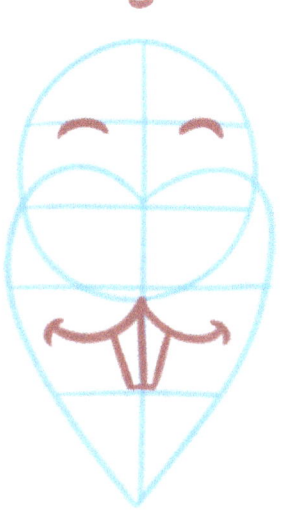

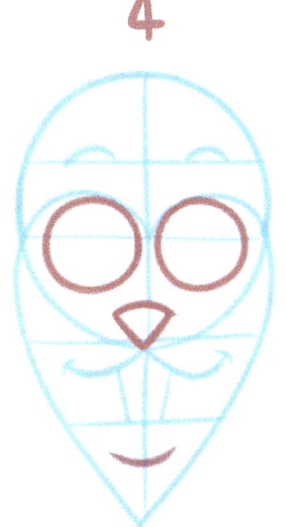

STEP 4

NOW ADD CIRCLES FOR HIS GLASSES, AN UPSIDEDOWN TRIANGLE FOR HIS NOSE AND A LINE FOR HIS CHIN.

STEP 5

NOW DRAW TWO BIG CIRCLES AND A SMALLER CIRCLE FOR THE EARS AND HAIR. AND ADD THE ARMS AND THE NOSE PIECE FOR HIS CLASSES.

STEP 6

NOW ADD THE HAIR IN THE EARS, WHISKERS AND THE FUR ON HIS COAT.

STEP 7

YOUR DRAWING SHOULD LOOK SIMILAR TO THIS.

STEP 8

FINALLY USE A PEN TO DRAW OVER THE TOP OF YOUR SKETCH. WAIT FOR THE INK TO DRY AND ERASE THE PENCIL LINES. WELL DONE!

WORD SEARCH

```
E T S E M O U S E Y
N K P F B X U T O S
C T A A M I U H A Y
R Q S C N E G M U Y
I T S A K A T G N M
T N K F U S T N E R
T T A A I R O O G R
E E J R M N U S N E
R E H A G W U G E E
S C H U M R O E E Y
```

1. Christmas
2. Mouse
3. Cake
4. Nonny
5. Panatone
6. Critters
7. Itsa
8. Bigger
9. Fae
10. Hum

DOT TO DOT!

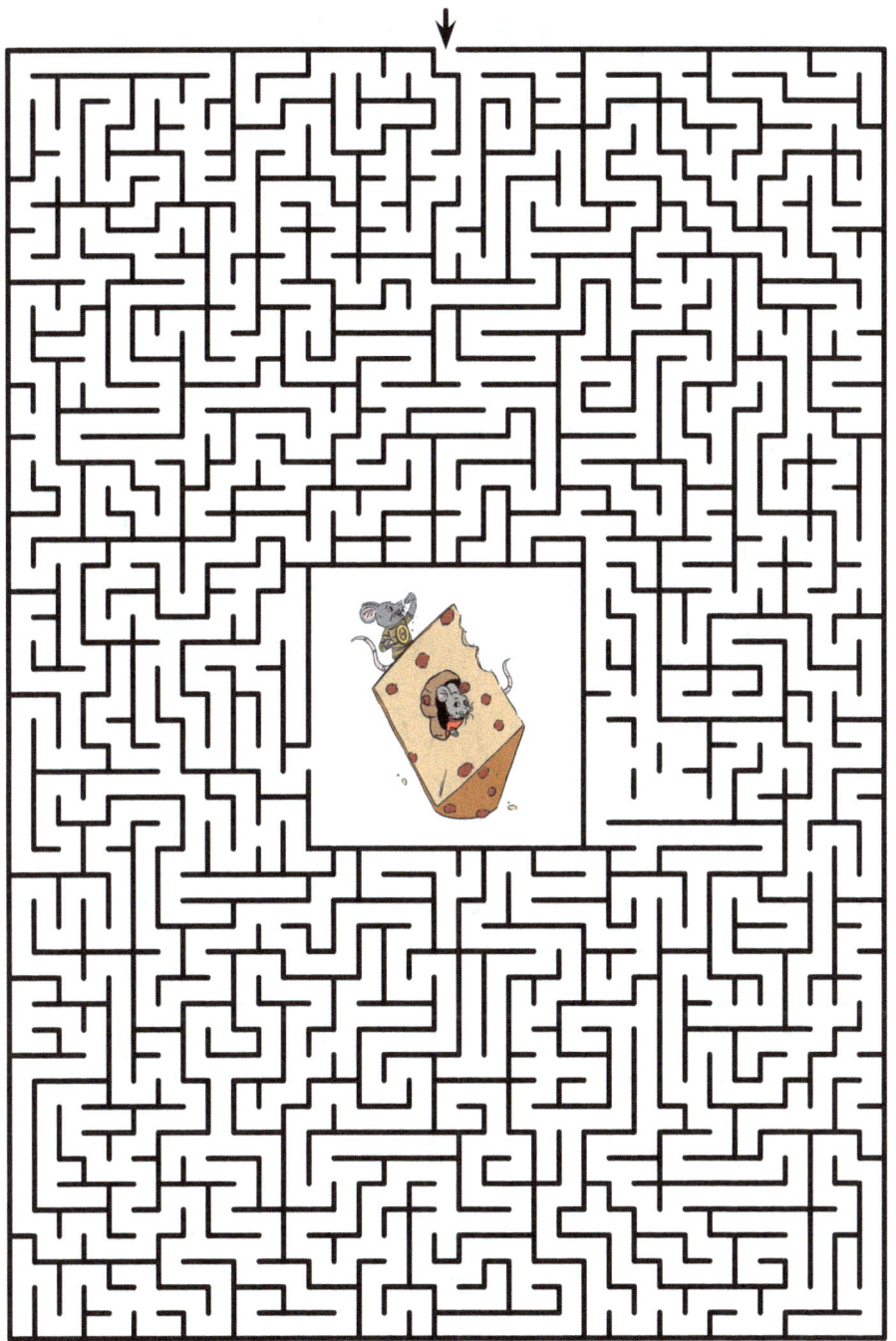

EXTRA SPECIAL THANKS TO OUR WONDERFUL YOUNG READER-REVIEWERS!

- Kal
- Luke Brincat
- Scarlett Bull
- Hayden Burton
- Xander Burton
- Amillie Carman
- Freddie Carman
- Benji Cassidy
- Daniel Cassidy
- Thomas Cassidy
- Ethan Dale
- Oscar Dale
- Alison Kam
- Andriani Kyriacou
- Axel Kyriacou
- Lowri Fon Richards
- Harrison Sessions
- Jacob Soussan

For your chance to be a featured young reader-reviewer make sure you are signed up to our mailing list.

PARENTS SIGN UP & DOWNLOAD YOUR FREE COLOUR-IN ITSA MOUSE ACTIVITY PACK FOR YOUR KIDS!

WHATS IN THE PACK?

- An **Itsa Mouse** book cover colouring sheet
- An **Itsa Mouse** print & play board game
- An **Itsa Mouse** foldable mini-comic colouring book
- An **Itsa Mouse** character mouse-mask

Visit: www.100percentpublishing.com/activitypack

www.ingramcontent.com/pod-product-compliance
Lightning Source LLC
Chambersburg PA
CBHW071025080526
44587CB00015B/2500